Beautiful Easter

TO:

FROM:

Easter
memories
warm the soul!

Joy Yizante

Easter spells out beauty, the rare beauty of new life

S.D. Gordon

The Easter egg symbolizes our ability to break out of the hardened protective shell we've surrounded ourselves with

Siobhan Shaw

Easter is the demonstration of God that life is essentially spiritual and timeless

Oscar Wilde

The great gift of Easter
is hope

Basil Hume

The story of Easter is the story of God's wonderful window of divine surprise

Carl Knudsen

The very first Easter
taught us this: that life
never ends and love
never dies

Kate McGahan

Easter says you can put truth in a grave, but it won't stay there

Clarence W. Hall

Easter is the only time when it's perfectly safe to put all your eggs in one basket

Evan Esar

There would be no Christmas if there was no Easter

Gordon B. Hinckley

For I remember it is Easter morn, and life and love and peace are all new born

Alice Freeman Palmer

Egg hunts are proof that your children can find things when they really want to

Unknown

EGG
HUNT

To a Christian, Easter Sunday means everything, when we celebrate the resurrection of Jesus Christ

Bernhard Langer

On Easter Day the veil between time and eternity thins to gossamer

Douglas Horton

Easter is meant to be a symbol of hope, renewal, and new life

Janine di Giovanni

The great gift of
Easter is hope

Basil C. Hume

April hath put a spirit of youth in everything

William Shakespeare

That is one good thing about this world there are always sure to be more springs

L.M Montgomery

A true friend is someone
who thinks you're a good
egg, even if you're cracked

Bernard Meltzer